DEFENDING OUR NATION

HOMELAND SECURITY

Series Titles

DEFENDING OUR NATION

HOMELAND SECURITY

FOREWORD BY
MANNY GOMEZ, ESQ., SECURITY AND TERRORISM EXPERT

BY
MICHAEL KERRIGAN

MASON CREST

Mason Crest
450 Parkway Drive, Suite D
Broomall, PA 19008
www.masoncrest.com

Printed in the United States of America
First printing
9 8 7 6 5 4 3 2 1

Series ISBN: 978-1-4222-3759-5
Hardcover ISBN: 978-1-4222-3767-0
ebook ISBN: 978-1-4222-8023-2

Library of Congress Cataloging-in-Publication Data

Names: Kerrigan, Michael, 1959- author.
Title: Homeland Security / foreword By Manny Gomez, Esq., Security And Terrorism Expert; by Michael Kerrigan.
Other titles: Department of Homeland Security
Description: Broomall, Pennsylvania : Mason Crest, [2018] | Series: Defending our nation | Includes index.
Identifiers: LCCN 2016053123| ISBN 9781422237670 (hardback) | ISBN
  9781422237595 (series) | ISBN 9781422280232 (ebook)
Subjects: LCSH: United States. Department of Homeland Security--Juvenile
  literature. | Terrorism--United States--Prevention--Juvenile literature. |
  National security--United States--Juvenile literature. | Civil
  defense--United States--Juvenile literature.
Classification: LCC HV6432 .K46 2018 | DDC 353.30973--dc23

Developed and Produced by Print Matters Productions, Inc.
(www.printmattersinc.com)
Cover and Interior Design by Bill Madrid, Madrid Design
Additional Text by Kelly Kagamas Tomkies

CONTENTS

KEY ICONS TO LOOK FOR:

Words to understand: These words with their easy-to-understand definitions will increase the reader's understanding of the text while building vocabulary skills.

Sidebars: This boxed material within the main text allows readers to build knowledge, gain insights, explore possibilities, and broaden their perspectives by weaving together additional information to provide realistic and holistic perspectives.

Educational Videos: Readers can view videos by scanning our QR codes, providing them with additional educational content to supplement the text. Examples include news coverage, moments in history, speeches, iconic sports moments and much more!

Text-dependent questions: These questions send the reader back to the text for more careful attention to the evidence presented there.

Research projects: Readers are pointed toward areas of further inquiry connected to each chapter. Suggestions are provided for projects that encourage deeper research and analysis.

Series glossary of key terms: This back-of-the book glossary contains terminology used throughout this series. Words found here increase the reader's ability to read and comprehend higher-level books and articles in this field.

FOREWORD

VIGILANCE

We live in a world where we have to have a constant state of awareness—about our surroundings and who is around us. Law enforcement and the intelligence community cannot predict or stop the next terrorist attack alone. They need the citizenry of America, of the world, to act as a force multiplier in order to help deter, detect, and ultimately defeat a terrorist attack.

Technology is ever evolving and is a great weapon in the fight against terrorism. We have facial recognition, we have technology that is able to detect electronic communications through algorithms that may be related to terrorist activity—we also have drones that could spy on communities and bomb them without them ever knowing that a drone was there and with no cost of life to us.

But ultimately it's human intelligence and inside information that will help defeat a potential attack. It's people being aware of what's going on around them: if a family member, neighbor, coworker has suddenly changed in a manner where he or she is suddenly spouting violent anti-Western rhetoric or radical Islamic fundamentalism, those who notice it have a duty to report it to authorities so that they can do a proper investigation.

In turn, the trend since 9/11 has been for international communication as well as federal and local communication. Gone are the days when law enforcement or intelligence organizations kept information to themselves and didn't dare share it for fear that it might compromise the integrity of the information or for fear that the other organization would get equal credit. So the NYPD wouldn't tell anything to the FBI, the FBI wouldn't tell the CIA, and the CIA wouldn't tell the British counterintelligence agency, MI6, as an example. Improved as things are, we could do better.

We also have to improve global propaganda. Instead of dropping bombs, drop education on individuals who are even considering joining ISIS. Education is salvation. We have the greatest production means in the world through Hollywood and so on, so why don't we match ISIS materials? We tried it once but the government itself tried to produce it. This is something that should definitely be privatized. We also need to match the energy of cyber attackers—and we need savvy youth for that.

There are numerous ways that you could help in the fight against terror—joining law enforcement, the military, or not-for-profit organizations like the Peace Corps. If making the world a safer place appeals to you, draw on your particular strengths and put them to use where they are needed. But everybody should serve and be part of this global fight against terrorism in some small way. Certainly, everybody should be a part of the fight by simply being aware of their surroundings and knowing when something is not right and acting on that sense. In the investigation after most successful attacks, we know that somebody or some persons or people knew that there was something wrong with the person or persons who perpetrated the attack. Although it feels awkward to tell the authorities that you believe somebody is acting suspicious and may be a terrorist sympathizer or even a terrorist, we have a higher duty not only to society as a whole but to our family, friends, and ultimately ourselves to do something to ultimately stop the next attack.

It's not *if* there is going to be another attack, but where, when, and how. So being vigilant and being proactive are the orders of the day.

Manny Gomez, Esq.
President of MG Security Services,
Chairman of the National Law Enforcement Association,
former FBI Special Agent, U.S. Marine, and NYPD Sergeant

CHAPTER 1
THE CHALLENGE

On September 11, 2001, the New York City skyline was forever changed. The terrorist attacks on the United States left its mark but we vowed to fight—and continue to do so—against those responsible.

Officially, the 21st century began on January 1, 2001, but in hindsight, the months that followed seemed an interlude falling outside of time. The century was nine months old when, out of the blue sky of a bright fall morning, terror came rushing from the sky to announce that a new historical era had begun.

The hideous symbolism of the outrage of September 11, 2001, was unmistakable: the twin towers of the World Trade Center were recognizable around the world as an image of the economic energy and enterprise of the United States. The Pentagon, in Washington, DC, was, and remains, the headquarters of the armed forces of the greatest military power the world has ever seen. There was nothing symbolic, however, about the thousands of innocent lives lost, the countless others injured, the grief of their families, or the pain of the United States as a whole.

The terrorist fanatics of Al Qaeda had hurled down a bloody challenge to the world's greatest democracy. Would it now collapse like a stricken skyscraper, or stand firm for freedom and justice? The global superpower had suddenly become vulnerable. How was it now to protect itself against an enemy who followed none of the old rules?

President George W. Bush believed that the United States did have the resources and courage to fight back against terror. He recognized, however, that the struggle would call for new strategies, new attitudes, and new ways of working. With this end in mind, he established the Department of Homeland Security to coordinate the response of the many different agencies responsible for guaranteeing the safety of Americans.

Words to Understand

Anti-Semitism: Hatred of Jewish people.

Fascism: Form of government ruled by a harsh dictator who controls the lives of the people.

Superpower: Extremely powerful nation.

A World Power

The 20th century ended with the United States acknowledged as the world's unrivaled **superpower**, its peace and prosperity apparently assured. It is important to remember, as we enter what are likely to be difficult and dangerous times, that America has fought for its freedoms—and those of other people around the world—many times before.

The United States was born from conflict when American colonists forcibly broke away from the British. Their freedom was fought for by the first citizen militias, the direct ancestors of our modern National Guard. Subsequently, the new country would have to defend its independence on the field of battle several times in the course of the 19th century. Indeed, it fought wars not only with Britain but also with France, Mexico, and Spain. Democracy has always had to be defended.

This belief propelled the United States onto the world stage in 1917, intervening to bring an end to the bloody stalemate of World War I. President Woodrow Wilson had, for some time, tried using diplomatic influence to end the carnage of the trenches; when these attempts failed, he felt the country had no alternative but action. The aggressive militarism of the kaiser's Germany

The carnage in the trenches may have been hard to bear in World War I, but first aid stations were set up to help the wounded, as shown in this 1918 photo.

had to be resisted, Americans felt—and they volunteered to fight for the freedom of Europe in the hundreds of thousands.

Within a generation, Germany was on the march again, this time under the ruthless leadership of the dictator Adolf Hitler. With his creed of nationalistic hatred, he succeeded in mobilizing the mass of ordinary Germans, demoralized as they were by the years of economic stagnation and political powerlessness that had followed Germany's defeat in 1918. The Jews, said the leader of the National Socialist (Nazi) Party, were the great sickness in German society, the source of all the country's many woes. Without the Jews, he promised, Germany would be able to assume its rightful place in the world: **anti-Semitism** became the great cause around which Germans rallied.

With its contempt for the idea of debate or disagreement and for the legal niceties of the electoral process, **fascism** was a political system that was the exact opposite of democracy. Yet, along with other fascist strongmen—most famously Benito Mussolini in Italy—Hitler did seem to be speaking for the "little guy" in the street. Hence the huge tide of popular support, which bore Germany and Italy along as they set out to bring the whole of Europe under their control.

On the other side of the world, meanwhile, military rulers in Japan were determined to extend their country's rule throughout the Pacific region—their alliance with fascist Europe was the original "axis of evil." As Hitler's henchmen set in motion

On October 25, 1936, an alliance was declared between Italy and Germany. Here, Italian dictator Benito Mussolini (left) shows his support for German dictator Adolf Hitler (right) during his regime.

their final solution to the "Jewish problem," Japanese forces were massacring men, women, and children in China and Korea.

Again, the United States sought at first to find a way to peace through quiet intervention behind the scenes. However, the attack on Pearl Harbor on December 7, 1941, made such detachment impossible. Forced to fight for freedom in the world, the United States did not shirk the task. Indeed, many feel that the nation came of age in the four-year struggle that ensued.

The Pearl Harbor naval base and U.S.S. Shaw ablaze in the distance after the Japanese attack.

The Cold War

The United States emerged from World War II in 1945 as a superpower. So, too, however, did another nation of a different kind: the Union of Soviet Socialist Republics, or USSR.

In 1917, Russian revolutionaries had overthrown the oppressive rule of the old emperors, or czars, only to establish an even more ferocious tyranny in its place—Communism. Murdering their political opponents, or dispatching them to die in distant labor camps, the Communists took an iron grip on every area of Soviet life. Businessmen and entrepreneurs (even hard-working peasants) were accused of exploiting their workers and were branded "class enemies," becoming the social scapegoats that the Jews had been for Nazi Germany.

The longer-term effects of this policy would eventually prove catastrophic—without men and women of initiative and energy, the USSR was economically doomed. However, in the immediate term, it created cohesion and a sense of social purpose. Hitler's invasion of Russia in 1941 and the bitter fighting of the "Great Patriotic War" that followed brought the whole country into line behind its leader, Joseph Stalin. His final victory in that fearful conflict lent his rule an air of legitimacy in the eyes of many Soviets, assuring the survival of a regime combining monstrous evil with the most abject economic incompetence.

Having thrown back the German invaders from their territories, Stalin's forces proceeded to "liberate" the German-occupied states of Eastern Europe, turning Poland, Czechoslovakia, Hungary, Romania, and the eastern half of Germany into Communist states. Only the presence of American and British armies prevented the wholesale annexation of Germany.

In the years that followed, the Soviet Union cemented its hold behind what British statesman Winston Churchill called the "Iron Curtain." The United States was forced into an ever-escalating arms race to protect itself and its democratic allies against the Communist threat. This uncomfortable confrontation between East and West, known as the Cold War, stopped short of all-out conflict between the superpowers, but a number of "proxy wars" were fought in various third-world countries. In the Korean War (1950–1953) and in the Vietnam War (1964–1974), U.S. forces were compelled to take action on the ground to defend democratic nations against invasion by satellite states of the Soviet Union.

In time, however, the costs of the arms race proved too much for a Communist "command economy," in which bureaucratic organization proved no substitute for the entrepreneurial spirit that had made the U.S. economy so strong. The Soviets' invasion of Afghanistan in 1979 to prop up a "puppet" government under pressure was to prove one expansionist measure too many. With its forces mired in an unwinnable war and its ramshackle economy straining to cope, the USSR was brought slowly but surely to its knees in the decade that followed.

Living with Terror

The threat of terrorism has been one of the realities of European life for many years. The troubles of Northern Ireland have often spilled over onto the streets of mainland Britain. Terrorists representing the Irish Republican Army (IRA) have attacked targets ranging from British Army recruiting offices to train stations, shopping malls, office buildings, tourist sites, and crowded bars in London and other cities.

There have been similar problems in Spain, where members of the separatist group ETA have been trying to bomb and assassinate their way to independence for the northerly Basque country. (ETA stands for Euskadi Ta Askatasuna, which means Basque Homeland and Freedom.)

Whatever the levels of "soft" support for national causes, in neither Northern Ireland nor the Basque country could the terrorists claim to be acting for the people as a whole. Nor could they claim to have succeeded in intimidating the populations they have attacked over a period of decades. For the most part, civilian populations have learned to live with the dangers posed by terrorist extremists. And any political advances that have been made, have been made by discussion and debate.

The Berlin Wall was a symbol of Communism for nearly 30 years. A section of the wall was placed directly in front of Germany's famous landmark—the Brandenburg Gate. Today, many gather at this landmark to celebrate the destruction of the Berlin Wall.

American Ascendancy

The demolition of the Berlin Wall by cheering crowds in November 1989 was the emblematic moment in the fall of Communism. For almost 30 years this structure separated East Berliners from their fellow citizens and relatives in the West. American culture was now recognized and sought after around the world. It was popularly exemplified by Mickey Mouse, McDonald's, and Michael Jackson. It represented the Western lifestyle so many people had been denied, but to which they had always secretly aspired.

Yet even amid the euphoria and the globalization of U.S. culture, there were signs that peace was under threat. One of the newly liberated countries, Yugoslavia, was an unhappy confederation of long-standing antagonistic nations in the Balkan region of southeastern Europe. Held

Three U.S. Army soldiers from the 11th Air Defense Artillery Brigade in 2006 during Operation Desert Storm.

together only by Communist force, Yugoslavia responded to its new freedom by spiraling into bitter conflict. Elsewhere, there were reminders that Communism might not be the only threat to freedom and peace when Saddam Hussein's Iraqi forces invaded Kuwait at the end of 1990.

As we have seen, however, the United States had learned the hard way of the need to arm itself for peace. Through the tense decades of the Cold War, it had developed the capacity to bring overwhelming force to bear on any state that sought to upset the international order. Serbia, bent on conquest in the Balkans, was to discover this at its own cost; as indeed was Saddam Hussein in the Gulf War of 1991.

New Realities

But states were no longer the only organizations to be acting on the world stage. International terrorism had been on the rise since the 1960s. The most notorious incidents of this kind were the "skyjackings" conducted by Palestinians protesting Israeli occupation of their lands. Aimed at bringing their grievances to the attention of the world, the hijacking of civilian airliners tested to the very limits the notion that "any publicity is good publicity"—and, in time, the practice was abandoned by the Palestinians.

The methods of terrorism were, however, eagerly embraced by another generation of even more fanatical fighters as a new wave of Islamic fundamentalism swept across the Middle East. Where earlier generations of Arabs were motivated by a mood of nationalism—a desire to be independent from the domination of the rich and powerful countries of the West—the fundamentalists spurn what they regard as ungodly and inglorious half-measures. For them, nothing is more important than Islam. Indeed, they draw inspiration from a literal-minded interpretation of the thoughts of the Prophet Muhammad as recorded in the Koran, and seek to sweep away all signs of modernity and Westernization—including the state of Israel—from the Middle East. As many scholars have pointed out, Islamic fundamentalism may be expressed as religious fervor, but many Muslims feel a more worldly resentment toward an affluent Western consumer culture from which they feel excluded.

Although fundamentalist groups like ISIS and Al Qaeda may work with "rogue states" in the furtherance of their cause, they scorn the artificial boundaries appointed by politics. Their identity is intrinsically transnational, owing no allegiance to any one government, while their membership may be drawn from Muslim communities across the Islamic world. This makes them a particularly elusive enemy. For the very reason that they cannot command the organizational resources of the centralized state, they do not have the sort of well-defined structure that can easily be identified and then destroyed. Al Qaeda, for instance, is believed to operate in over 40 countries and to be so loosely constituted that the destruction of one cell would have little impact on the organization as a whole.

It is worth remembering that terrorism is not just a threat from outside. On April 19, 1995, a huge truck bomb blew away the entire front of Oklahoma City's Murrah Building—and destroyed America's peace of mind. This attack cost the lives of 168 men, women, and children, and another 500 were injured, many quite seriously. It was, at this point, the most serious terrorist attack on U.S. soil—and it was the work not of foreign terrorists, but of self-styled "patriots."

A memorial in Oklahoma City to remember the victims of the bombing of the Murrah Building.

Americans were shaken to learn that some individuals consider the federal government of the United States to be the enemy. For Timothy McVeigh, a white supremacist and one of the men responsible for the bombing, the government is an alien "occupying force." The government's offense, as far as the white supremacist right is concerned, is to admit immigrants to the country and to promote the welfare of those nonwhite groups already here (including Jews, African Americans, and Hispanics). Rather than protecting white Americans from the encroachments of such groups, the federal government places restrictions on the rights of these "patriots" to carry arms. Outlandish as it may sound, the similarities between white and Islamic fundamentalist groups are clear. Both movements rationalize the rage of groups who feel marginalized by the normal political processes of their countries. And, like the racist frenzy of the Nazis, the anger of the white supremacists stems from a profound sense that a people who should be privileged by destiny are, in reality, living impoverished and powerless lives.

New Risks

Used in both the first World Trade Center attack of 1993 and the Oklahoma City blast two years later, bombs are, unfortunately, only the first weapons in the terrorist **armory**. They are also among the least potent. Deadly as their consequences often are, their range is limited and their effects immediate. In recent years, however, a range of more insidious weapons has become available. There are growing fears about the possibility of **cyberterrorism** or the use of chemical or biological weapons. The prospect of **bioterrorism** is peculiarly frightening because its action is both invisible and delayed, and its effects may be carried far and wide among the population by secondary infection.

Despite the comparatively small number of actual casualties, the anthrax attacks that followed the atrocities of September 11, 2001, were profoundly disturbing—and it makes little difference whether they were the work of a lone screwball or an international terrorist conspiracy. Whoever was behind them, they highlighted the potential for panic and widespread disruption, and the inadequacy of the preventive procedures that were then in place.

Although a minor situation in comparison to the World Trade Center and Pentagon attacks, the anthrax scare still served as a warning to America. The world today is a dangerous place. Our armed forces, although formidable, cannot be expected to guarantee our protection against enemies who may strike by any means. Tactics such as suicide bombings and driving trucks into crowds seem to have gained prevalence by the jihadist group ISIS in the 2010s.

Text-Dependent Questions

1. Why did President George W. Bush organize the Department of Homeland Security?
2. What forced the United States to participate in World War II?
3. What was the Cold War?

Research Projects

1. What is bioterrorism and what groups are using this tactic? How is the Department of Homeland Security battling this tactic?
2. Research the Oklahoma City bombing. How and why was the attack carried out? What improvements in security were enacted afterward?

CHAPTER 2
THE RESPONSE

In the aftermath of 9/11, airports around the world increased their security protocols. The customs station in Ulan-Ude, Buryatia, Russia includes the vigorous scanning of luggage.

There is no denying the fact that the outrages of September 11, 2001, took the United States by surprise—and hit the world's most powerful nation where it hurt. Americans reeled from the shock, profoundly perplexed. What had caused this? And what was to be the response?

Defenseless and innocent civilians found themselves on a frontline of someone else's making. In a matter of hours, and on a scale never before seen, thousands had died. The nation was eager to strike back, but unsure where the blow should fall. Such frustration could easily have led to demoralization and paranoia. True, the valor of the rescue services was inspirational, but there was a real danger that Americans might lose their nerve at this crucial moment. The greatest military machine the world has ever seen and its formidable intelligence apparatus had been powerless against a few determined terrorists armed only with simple blades.

Calm courage prevailed. Establishing the Department of Homeland Security, the president acknowledged the gravity of the threat, but at the same time asserted his complete confidence in the nation's ability to confront it. An umbrella organization, the office has a role, not to create new capabilities for our defense, but to coordinate the work of existing agencies. The United States already has the material and human resources necessary for its own defense; the task of the new office is to bring them to battle-readiness.

Words to Understand

Decontamination: Remove dirty or dangerous substances from a person or object.

Improvised: Make or create something using whatever materials are available.

Toxin: Poisonous substance.

Operation Noble Eagle

The scrambling of F-16 fighters in the immediate aftermath of the terrorist attacks was of great symbolic importance. The sight of them patrolling the skies above our major cities was an important show of strength—for the benefit both of the American people and of their enemies. These fighters could indeed have prevented a repetition of the World Trade Center or Pentagon attacks, although to shoot down an airliner full of passengers would be, by any standard, a desperate measure.

F-16 fighter jets protecting U.S. cities.

Of more practical significance, perhaps, was the mobilization of the National Guard to beef up airport security. Again, this sent a message both to America itself and to its enemies in the outside world: the people of the United States are resolved to defend themselves, standing by the cause of freedom as they have done so many times before. The involvement of the National Guard was especially crucial, representing as it did a return to the oldest traditions of the nation. Directly descended from those citizen militias that defended the first European settlers against attack, and which afterward drove the British colonists from these shores, the National Guard is a neighborhood-based force of ordinary Americans who have sworn to defend their home communities. By rallying to the flag at this moment, ordinary Americans proclaimed their readiness to come to the defense of their homeland—and sent a message of symbolic importance that is more profound than the deployment of regular forces would have implied.

Not that our armed forces were idle. The Army, Air Force, Marines, and Navy were soon in action, taking the fight to Al Qaeda in the mountains and cave complexes of Afghanistan. But the smashing of the terrorists and their Taliban protectors on the ground has overshadowed what may, in time, prove to have been a far more significant development: the establishment of the Department of Homeland Security under Governor Tom Ridge.

Nevada Guardmembers patrol the baggage claim area at McCarran International Airport.

Operation Noble Eagle's training patrol.

The Man Of The Moment

On October 8, 2001, Governor Tom Ridge of Pennsylvania was sworn in as director of the president's new Department of Homeland Security. Ridge had come a long way from his working-class roots in Pittsburgh's Steel Valley. After gaining a scholarship to Harvard in 1967, he interrupted his law studies to serve in Vietnam, where he was decorated for valor. Back home in America, politics proved to be a battlefield of a different sort, but Ridge has consistently shown himself to be a tough, yet fair-minded, fighter. At his swearing in, he spelled out the principles he planned to introduce, arguing that what was required was not a new set of skills or capabilities but the rediscovery and redirection of a spirit that had stood America in good stead throughout its history:

"Americans should find comfort in knowing that millions of their fellow citizens are working every day to ensure our security at every level—federal, state, county, municipal. These are dedicated professionals who are good at what they do. I've seen it up close, as governor of Pennsylvania.

"But there may be gaps in the system. The job of the Department of Homeland Security will be to identify those gaps and work to close them. The size and scope of this challenge are immense. The president's executive order states that we must detect, prepare for, prevent, protect against, respond to, and recover from terrorist attacks, an extraordinary mission. But we will carry it out. . . .

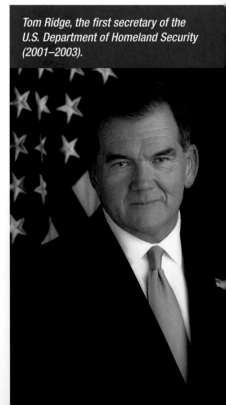

Tom Ridge, the first secretary of the U.S. Department of Homeland Security (2001–2003).

"It's called Homeland Security. While the effort will begin here, it will require the involvement of Americans at every level. Everyone in the homeland must play a part. I ask the American people for their patience, their awareness, and their resolve. This job calls for a national effort. We've seen it before, whether it was building the transcontinental railroad, fighting World War II, or putting a man on the moon."

Needles in Haystacks

Almost 500 million people a year enter America through established border crossings; many thousands more slip across illegally or hop ashore at unobserved landing places. Any one of these visitors could be carrying a weapon of mass destruction, which might be as small as a scent bottle—might, indeed, even be a scent bottle full of biotoxin for aerosol dispersion. Any one of the more than 120 million passenger vehicles that enter the country each year could have a "suitcase bomb" in the trunk: an **improvised** nuclear device to be feared as a source of radiation rather than for the force of its blast.

However hard we watch our 7,000 miles (11,272 km) of land frontier and our many thousands more of coastline, how are we to apprehend those terrorists—whether foreign or homegrown—already in our midst? The fear could paralyze us if we let it. The answer is to combine vigilance with calm, for these comings and goings are vital to the life of the nation. If we are not to travel or admit visitors or allow the free-flowing importation or distribution of goods, we will effectively be surrendering, doing the work of the terrorists for them.

Warning signs, similar to this, can be seen at international boundaries between the United States and Canada.

"There are some things we can do immediately, and we will. Others will take more time. But we will find something for every American to do. My friends in the Army Corps of Engineers remind me of their motto, 'The difficult, we do immediately. The impossible takes a little longer.'"

In 2013, Jeh Charles Johnson was appointed Secretary of Homeland Security. DHS is now the third largest department of the U.S. government, with a workforce of 229,000 employees. Prior to becoming Secretary, Johnson was General Counsel of the Department of Defense.

U.S. Department o

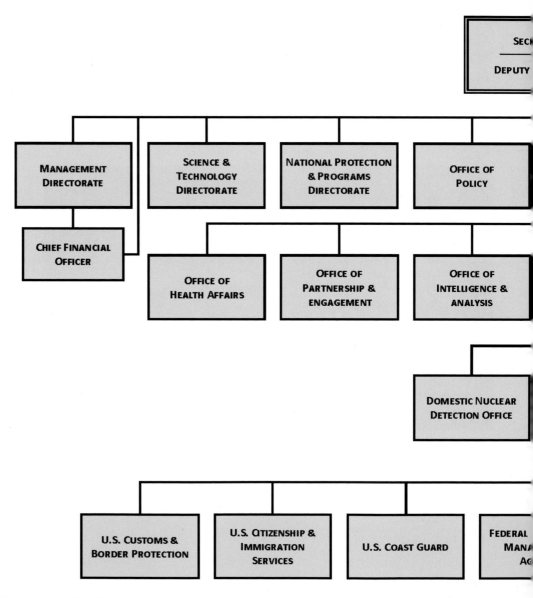

SEC[
DEPUTY

MANAGEMENT DIRECTORATE

SCIENCE & TECHNOLOGY DIRECTORATE

NATIONAL PROTECTION & PROGRAMS DIRECTORATE

OFFICE OF POLICY

CHIEF FINANCIAL OFFICER

OFFICE OF HEALTH AFFAIRS

OFFICE OF PARTNERSHIP & ENGAGEMENT

OFFICE OF INTELLIGENCE & ANALYSIS

DOMESTIC NUCLEAR DETECTION OFFICE

U.S. CUSTOMS & BORDER PROTECTION

U.S. CITIZENSHIP & IMMIGRATION SERVICES

U.S. COAST GUARD

FEDERAL MANA AG

Homeland Security

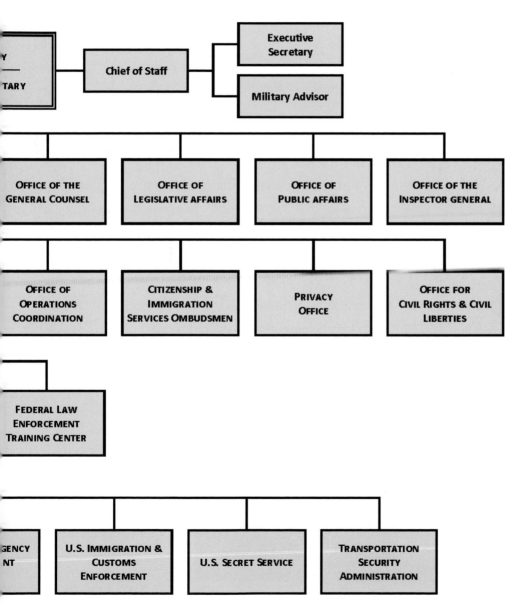

- Chief of Staff
  - Executive Secretary
  - Military Advisor

- OFFICE OF THE GENERAL COUNSEL
- OFFICE OF LEGISLATIVE AFFAIRS
- OFFICE OF PUBLIC AFFAIRS
- OFFICE OF THE INSPECTOR GENERAL

- OFFICE OF OPERATIONS COORDINATION
- CITIZENSHIP & IMMIGRATION SERVICES OMBUDSMEN
- PRIVACY OFFICE
- OFFICE FOR CIVIL RIGHTS & CIVIL LIBERTIES

- FEDERAL LAW ENFORCEMENT TRAINING CENTER

- U.S. IMMIGRATION & CUSTOMS ENFORCEMENT
- U.S. SECRET SERVICE
- TRANSPORTATION SECURITY ADMINISTRATION

A New Way of Thinking

The establishment of an administrative office may seem absurdly undramatic after the fearful inferno of September 11. Yet the creation of the Department of Homeland Security indicates the president's recognition that what was required in that situation might not necessarily be ever more, ever "smarter" firepower in the field. While high-tech weaponry has proved its value in Afghanistan and elsewhere, what was needed most immediately was a higher level of preparation and administrative control at home.

We must continue to be aware of the threat of biological attack. This has been a theoretical possibility for a long time now, but it has come to seem all too possible. Consider, for example, a biological attack by aerosol on a city subway. The weapon would be discreet—a perfume bottle or other small spray—and the attack itself might pass entirely unnoticed. The victims themselves, rushing commuters, might easily be unaware that they had been "hit," and several days might pass before they started feeling any ill effects. Even then, when they saw their doctor, the significance of their symptoms might escape notice. Meanwhile, they would unwittingly be passing on their infection to their families, friends, and fellow workers. In such a situation, we have to rethink what we understand by the word *defense*: an alert member of the public who spotted the attack as it happened or a nurse or doctor who was quick to see the signs thereafter would be of more value in such a situation than an aircraft carrier or a tank division.

Documentary on the terrorist attacks of 9/11.

The Department of Homeland Security Seal

The Department of Homeland Security seal was unveiled in June 2003, four months after DHS began formal operations as a standalone cabinet-level agency.

The seal is meant to symbolize the Department's mission—to prevent attacks and protect Americans—on the land, in the sea, and in the air.

The eagle's outstretched wings break through the inner circle into the outer ring to suggest that the Department of Homeland Security would break through traditional bureaucracy and perform government functions differently. In the tradition of the Great Seal of the United States, the eagle's talon on the left holds an olive branch with 13 leaves and 13 seeds while the eagle's talon on the right grasps 13 arrows.

Centered on the eagle's breast is a shield divided into three sections containing elements that represent the American homeland—air, land, and sea. The top element, a dark blue sky, contains 22 stars representing the original 22 entities that were brought together to form the department.

Managing the Fear

A psychologist at the U.S. Department of Veterans Affairs Medical Center, New York, Paul Ofman has studied the sort of mental stresses a bioterrorist attack may cause. The great problem is, he says, that with no warning, no loud explosion—indeed, no indication that an attack has taken place at all—individuals have no way of knowing whether or not they have been affected.

"Evidence that the tornado or hurricane has come and gone is pretty unambiguous," he told Scott Sleek of the American Psychological Association *Monitor.* "But when it's something that contaminates the air you breathe, when people don't really know what's going on, there's much more distress. Where is it? Where did it happen? When will it end? What are the long-term effects? All these questions raise the risk for panic."

Active Shooter Situations

The Department of Homeland Security has developed a program to assist businesses, government offices, and schools in preparing for and responding to an active shooter.

An active shooter is an individual actively engaged in killing or attempting to kill people in a confined and populated area; in most cases, active shooters use firearms(s) and there is no pattern or method to their selection of victims. Active shooter situations are unpredictable and evolve quickly. Because active shooter situations are often over within 10 to 15 minutes, before law enforcement arrives on the scene, individuals must be prepared both mentally and physically to deal with an active shooter situation.

DHS recommends the following best practices to prepare for and cope with an active shooter situation:

- Be aware of your environment and any possible dangers
- Take note of the two nearest exits in any facility you visit
- If you are in an office, stay there and secure the door
- If you are in a hallway, get into a room and secure the door
- As a last resort, attempt to take the active shooter down. When the shooter is at close range and you cannot flee, your chance of survival is much greater if you try to incapacitate him/her.

Handling an active shooter situation.

HOW TO RESPOND
WHEN AN ACTIVE SHOOTER IS IN YOUR VICINITY

QUICKLY DETERMINE THE MOST REASONABLE WAY TO PROTECT YOUR OWN LIFE. CUSTOMERS AND CLIENTS ARE LIKELY TO FOLLOW THE LEAD OF EMPLOYEES AND MANAGERS DURING AN ACTIVE SHOOTER SITUATION.

1. EVACUATE

- Have an escape route and plan in mind
- Leave your belongings behind
- Keep your hands visible

2. HIDE OUT

- Hide in an area out of the active shooter's view.
- Block entry to your hiding place and lock the doors

CALL 911 WHEN IT IS SAFE TO DO SO

3. TAKE ACTION

- As a last resort and only when your life is in imminent danger.
- Attempt to incapacitate the active shooter
- Act with physical aggression and throw items at the active shooter

HOW TO RESPOND
WHEN LAW ENFORCEMENT ARRIVES ON THE SCENE

1. HOW YOU SHOULD REACT WHEN LAW ENFORCEMENT ARRIVES:

- Remain calm, and follow officers' instructions
- Immediately raise hands and spread fingers
- Keep hands visible at all times
- Avoid making quick movements toward officers such as attempting to hold on to them for safety
- Avoid pointing, screaming and/or yelling
- Do not stop to ask officers for help or direction when evacuating, just proceed in the direction from which officers are entering the premises

2. INFORMATION YOU SHOULD PROVIDE TO LAW ENFORCEMENT OR 911 OPERATOR:

- Location of the active shooter
- Number of shooters, if more than one
- Physical description of shooter/s
- Number and type of weapons held by the shooter/s
- Number of potential victims at the location

RECOGNIZING SIGNS
OF POTENTIAL WORKPLACE VIOLENCE

AN ACTIVE SHOOTER MAY BE A CURRENT OR FORMER EMPLOYEE. ALERT YOUR HUMAN RESOURCES DEPARTMENT IF YOU BELIEVE AN EMPLOYEE EXHIBITS POTENTIALLY VIOLENT BEHAVIOR. INDICATORS OF POTENTIALLY VIOLENT BEHAVIOR MAY INCLUDE ONE OR MORE OF THE FOLLOWING:

- Increased use of alcohol and/or illegal drugs
- Unexplained increase in absenteeism, and/or vague physical complaints
- Depression/Withdrawal
- Increased severe mood swings, and noticeably unstable or emotional responses
- Increasingly talks of problems at home
- Increase in unsolicited comments about violence, firearms, and other dangerous weapons and violent crimes

Contact your building management or human resources department
for more information and training on active shooter response in your workplace.

It is not enough for us to be alert. We have to know what we are on the lookout for, and our emergency services have to be thoroughly schooled in the handling of every conceivable sort of emergency. Courage, admirable as it is, is no substitute for expertise; nor can energy and enthusiasm do the work of careful preparation. Some years ago, for example, a collaborative exercise was staged in which police officers, firefighters, and National Guard squads worked side by side to tackle a bioterrorist emergency. In an impressively well-oiled exercise, they moved in quickly and efficiently and had the whole area cleared of people and thoroughly washed down in a matter of minutes. This would have been the correct procedure in the aftermath of a chemical attack. In the case of a biological attack, it would have been a calamity because using water would have helped disperse the biological agent.

Our health care workers must be trained to recognize the early signs of a bioterrorist attack. The first symptoms of a fatal disease may be nothing worse than aching joints and a few sniffles. The sooner such diseases can be identified, the better the chance of successfully treating them—and slowing their spread.

All responders, not just medics, must learn to deal with the effects of panic, which can too easily turn a minor incident into a mass tragedy. There is no greater **toxin** than terror. When terrorists released sarin, a nerve gas, on the Tokyo subway in 1995, roughly 5,500 people needed medical treatment. The vast majority, however, turned out to have been suffering the effects of shock; only a handful had actually been affected by the gas itself. Law enforcement officers, firefighters, and other services are likely to find their relief efforts hampered by the mass hysteria that often follows incidents of this kind. The public must remember the importance of keeping calm whatever the danger.

While frontline emergency rescue workers are unlikely to flee screaming from the scene of an atrocity, this does not mean they are immune from the effects of panic. It can be extraordinarily hard to maintain efficient procedures amid a general atmosphere

After the 1995 sarin attacks in Japan, fire and police departments now take part in antiterrorism drills that simulate nerve gas attacks.

of hysteria, as responders to the 1995 Tokyo subway attack discovered. With panic-stricken people filling stairways and elevators, milling around subway entrances, and collapsing in the roadways outside, rescue workers had great difficulty reaching the site of the attack.

It takes discipline for operational effectiveness to be maintained in such circumstances—for which exercises can provide only partial preparation. Managing panic is among the most important aspects of emergency relief in a situation of this kind. Indeed, in some cases, it is as important as actual **decontamination**. Rescue services don't need the most expensive equipment, but they do need equipment that functions and will not buckle under the strain of a big emergency.

Departments around the world participate in terrorism drills to be better prepared for biological warfare.

Cooperation

The effects of public panic might be intensified by organizational difficulties. Confusion is almost inevitable when a number of different services are asked to collaborate under extreme pressure. Hence the need for the Department of Homeland Security, which oversees the work of 16 separate agencies. These range from the U.S. Citizenship and Immigration Services to the Domestic Nuclear Detection Office. More than 240,000 employees work to ensure the security of the United States.

Yet even when agencies are willing to cooperate, they may have their own—often quite different—ways of doing things. At the scene of a terrorist attack, compare the instincts of a law enforcement agency, such as a local police force or the FBI, with those of a rescue service, such as a fire department or a paramedic crew. For the former, this is a crime scene that must be protected and searched for evidence; for the latter, it is an outbreak to be suppressed, with casualties that must be cleared with all possible urgency.

Professor Loch Johnson of the University of Georgia has described America's antiterrorist establishment as a "bowl of spaghetti"—so many different agencies communicating (or not communicating) along a complicated chain of command. The task of the Department of Homeland Security is to make this bewildering array of organizations function as a single entity, pulling together in a single common cause: the defense and protection of the United States.

Effective Homeland Security is likely to be "homely" security: a matter of doing simple things efficiently. A clear chain of command will be far more important than any amount of high-tech weaponry, while all the intelligence information in the world will not help us if it cannot be communicated readily from one agency to another.

Text-Dependent Questions

1. How many people suffered the effects of the nerve gas sarin on a Tokyo subway in 1995?
2. How many separate agencies make up the Department of Homeland Security?
3. What is the primary task of the Department of Homeland Security?

Research Projects

1. When did the first director of DHS resign? What other leadership or government positions has he held since?
2. Research Operation Noble Eagle. What armed forces were involved? When did it begin and end? How was the DHS involved?

CHAPTER 3

IN THE FRONTLINE

The men and women of the The New York City Police Department is one of the best trained urban antiterrorist forces in the world.

The police officers and firefighters who ran into the wreckage of the World Trade Center to help their fellow New Yorkers were doing what they did every day—their duty. For too long, we have taken such everyday heroism for granted. Now we recognize the dangers of this work and realize that those dangers may increase.

On September 11, 2001, the spotlight fell on the first responders, those who routinely put their lives on the line. On that day, they risked their lives—and lost. As we embark upon an unpredictable, and probably protracted, War Against Terror, the work of first responders, which has always been dangerous, looks set to become even more so. All of us are now combatants in a war whose frontline runs through our city streets, our schools, our places of worship, our very homes. And in the forefront stand those men and women who have undertaken the protection of their communities and of America at large. Hence the Department of Homeland Security attaches great importance to the work of the various law enforcement and rescue services, and it is determined to lend them the fullest possible support.

A Nation on the Watch

Formerly with the Center for Defense Information in Washington, DC (an organization that merged with the Project on Government Oversight in 2012), retired U.S. Army Colonel Daniel Smith summed up the thinking of many experts when he told the *Christian Science Monitor* that ordinary Americans needed to "shed their daily self-absorption and become more aware of their surroundings." In an age when many people, even school students, carry cellular phones wherever they go, we could all play a vital role as "eyes and ears" of the authorities. Abandoned cars, suspicious packages—indeed "anything that seems out of place," says Smith, should be promptly reported. "It may not seem much, but it can make all the difference."

A new philosophy? Well, not exactly. These are the principles on which Neighborhood Watch has worked for over 30 years. Effectively relaunched on the back of the current concern for Homeland Security, this nationwide program of public vigilance enables every man, woman, and child to make a contribution to the defense of the nation.

Words to Understand

Competence: Ability to do something well.

Covert: Act done in a secret or hidden manner.

Mobilization: Act of mobilizing.

Heroes of the Hour

As she sat quietly in a Houston restaurant snatching a few minutes' break in a busy day, police officer Vanessa de la Garza almost fell out of her chair when a stranger walked up to offer her a torrent of congratulations. "I'm glad you're doing this job," said the stranger. "If no one else tells you today, let me be the one to say, 'Thank you for being a police officer.'" It was welcome praise, of course. Indeed, as Vanessa explained to the *Christian Science Monitor's* Abraham McLaughlin, she had been going through a "down" phase lately, wondering whether her work really made any difference, whether her career had any value.

The days and weeks following the cataclysm of September 11, 2001, were first and foremost a time of tragedy for first responders, as they mourned lost friends and realized that they too could have died. Yet it was also a time when the glamorous Manhattan hostess simply had to have a firefighter or two on the guest list for her party, and police officers were given standing ovations as they walked on patrol past outside cafes. The positive reaction spread far and wide throughout the United States, coming down many hundreds of miles away from Lower Manhattan. Sergeant Horace Nero of the Saint Petersburg, FL, Police Department, was flabbergasted to find kids coming up to him on the street and begging for his autograph.

But, despite the praise, America's 436,000 police officers and 186,000 sheriffs' officers have their feet firmly on the ground. No one could be more conscious of the mounting dangers and the increased workload they have brought. Officers appreciate the new respect they are shown by members of the public, who might previously have looked straight through them, but if the situation has its positive side, it has also undoubtedly brought more stress.

Part of the challenge is that they are now on the lookout for an entirely uncertain and unspecified threat. Matthew Webb, of the Saint Paul Police Department, told Minnesota Public Radio, "I can remember being assigned to actually be part of a detail where we watched one of our patrol houses and I remember asking my supervisor, 'What do you want me to watch for?' And he said, 'Well, I don't know!'"

The United States has more than a million firefighters, of whom around 750,000 are volunteers. Buckman called for an additional 75,000 full-time professionals to be taken on and trained after September 11. He also insisted on the need for enhanced equipment and training for existing officers, who might now find themselves having to tackle dangers they never envisaged—notably, chemical and biological weapons. This issue caused controversy in New York City, where, by the beginning of 2002, grief was giving way to anger as firefighters asked whether the eloquent tributes they had received were going to be matched by substantive support. This would have to range from protection against chemical and biological toxins to more effective radios; from better flashlights to special "crisis routes," which would let fire engines speed to the scene of an incident through the gridlocked city. Such measures, say spokesmen, are necessary not only to save the lives of firefighters but also to provide the best possible protection for members of the general public.

Another important enhancement is the National Data Exchange, commonly known as N-DEX. N-DEX is a system used nationally by law enforcement agencies to share data collected, including tips and leads. Computer programs are also in place to mine social media posts following major violent events to determine if the poster was actually at the event.

In 2008, local law enforcement gained an important tool for "connecting the dots" between data on people, places, and things that may seem unrelated in order to link investigations and investigators. N-DEx, a national repository of criminal justice records submitted by agencies from around the nation, provides criminal justice agencies with an online tool for sharing, searching, linking, and analyzing information across jurisdictional boundaries.

A Different Outlook

Battalion Chief John Norman, placed in charge of the New York City Fire Department's Special Operations section, admits that progress in preparing and protecting firefighters for terrorist emergencies has been too slow. For years, before the events of September 11, 2001, there were warnings of the risk of terrorist attack, but the danger never seemed quite immediate enough, and nothing was ever done. That is likely to change now, however, he told reporters from the New York Times: "September 11 woke a lot of people up." Money matters, he admits. Terrorists today can draw on huge resources; firefighters need the best of training and equipment if they are to stand in the frontline against them. Yet attitude may be just as important, he insists: "Awareness is the key. Treat everything as if it's the one that's going to kill you. . . . I think it's going to be harder to surprise us now." One of the major changes that has occurred in the aftermath of September 11 is the fact that it has become standard operating procedure for first responders across disciplines (firefighters and police, for example) to communicate with one another. Interoperability among first responders means they assign an event to a radio channel and work together during the event.

FEMA Fights Fires

A wildfire is a fire that rages out of control in the wilderness, like a forest or countryside. In 2015 the U.S. reported more than 68,000 wildfires that consumed nearly ten million acres. The U.S. Fire Administration, an entity of the U.S. Department of Homeland Security's Federal Emergency Management Agency (FEMA) coordinates closely with state, local, and tribal authorities and provides them with federal money to fight wildfires.

Human-caused climate change is thought to have almost doubled the number of acres burned in western United States wildfires during the last 30 years, according to a study published in the *Proceedings of the National Academy of Sciences of the United States of America* in October 2016.

The Medical Services

Doctors never saw themselves as soldiers before, but now, they, too, have to come to the defense of their homeland. There are 155,000 EMTs (emergency medical technicians) in the United States, and other terrorist attacks may bring them to the frontline, along with other health care workers. Indeed, they will be essential in the case of a **covert** bioterrorist attack.

An EMT team provides first aid on the street.

The alert nurse who puts two and two together and realizes that an apparently mundane miscellany of aches, pains, and sniffles adds up to something more sinister may quite easily end up saving hundreds—perhaps even thousands—of lives. "The ER nurse must maintain a high lovol of ouspicion all the time," says Jim Fenn of the Toledo Hospital, OH. "She must not be afraid to suggest to the physician some differential diagnoses that could indicate a biological attack, so at least they could rule that out." Again, the need is for vigilance—and better a false alarm than that a real attack be missed; sometimes the junior nurse might see something a senior doctor is too hurried or harassed to notice.

Some experts believe that our hospitals are our weakest point. Kim Jones is a registered nurse and is actively engaged in training hospital staff, police officers, and firefighters to work together in response to large-scale incidents. She told *Nurseweek* of her concerns that this sort of training had been neglected for far too long. In theory, hospitals are required to make provision for such emergencies, preparing incident plans and holding practice drills every six months. In practice, Jones remarked ruefully, too many managers have felt they had more important things to do. "Prior to September 11, most hospital administrators saw the disaster committee as just another annoying activity."

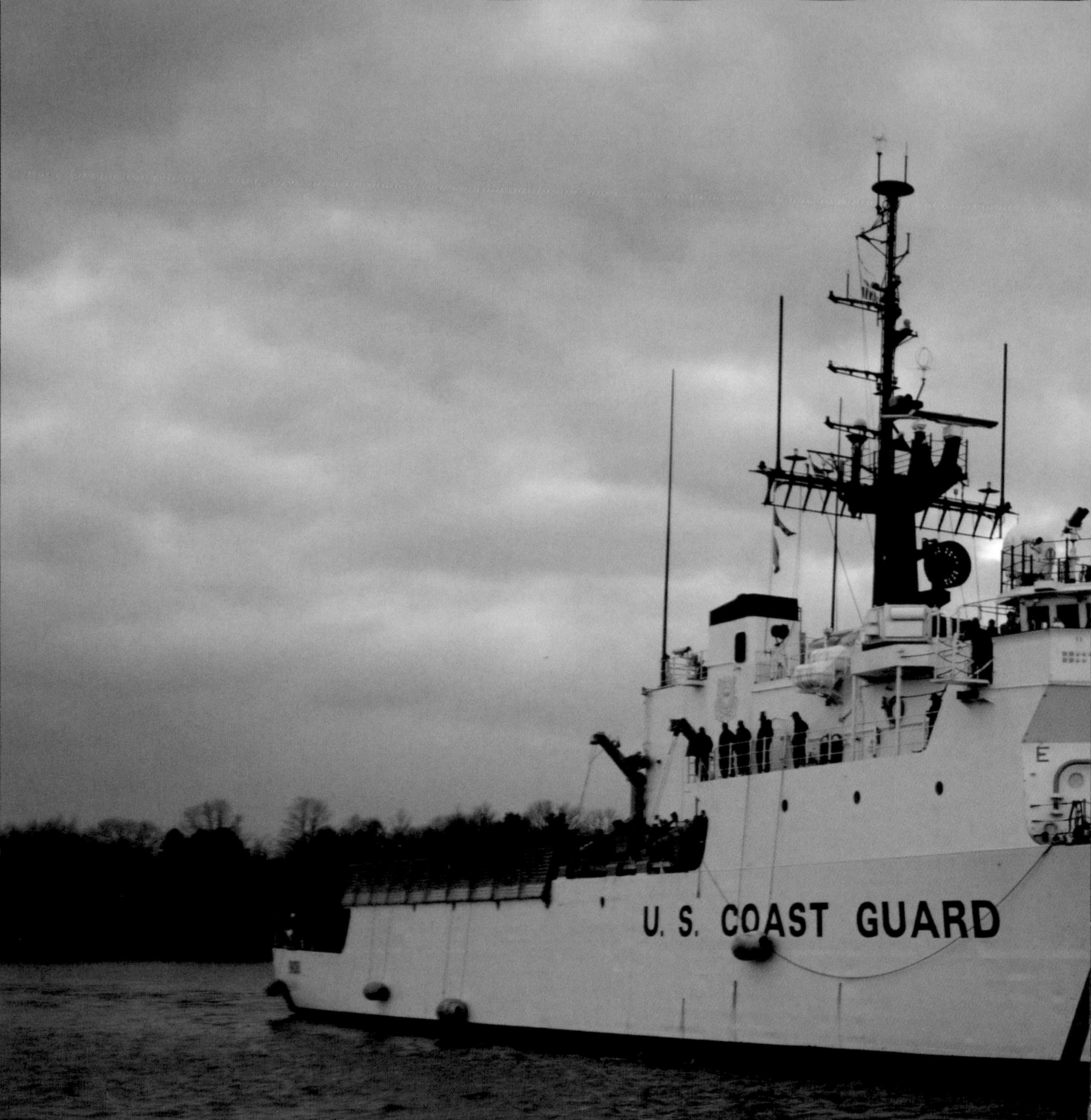
U.S. COAST GUARD

The U.S. Coast Guard, a branch of the Armed Services, is a crucial player in the fight against terrorism.

Resources were—as ever—a problem. Who wanted to invest in expensive decontamination facilities for attacks that would surely never happen? The money could be better spent on other equipment. With pressure to reduce costs, administrators never seemed to think it was a good time to stock up on antibiotics that, in all probability, would never be used. The attacks of September 11 jolted everyone out of their complacency, from the federal government downward. Five billion dollars in grants for hospital preparedness programs were proposed after September 11. Many local health authorities, like that of Los Angeles County, acted energetically to bring hospitals and health care workers up to speed.

Cooperation Is Key

Off Savannah, GA, the Coast Guard also stepped up its coastal patrols in the hours after the attacks of September 11. Charged with seeing to the protection of ports and harbors from South Carolina's Edisto River to the Florida border, the Coast Guard boarded all commercial vessels, screening crews and checking cargoes. But officers were fully aware that they were unlikely to stumble upon a wanted terrorist or a stash of weaponry themselves; their role was to help in a collective effort to put the pieces of the puzzle into a larger picture.

"Coordination is very, very important," Commander James McDonald of the Coast Guard told the *Savannah Morning News.* His officials were in constant touch with colleagues in the FBI, the Customs Service, the Immigration and Naturalization Service, the Georgia Ports Authority police, and the Savannah Police Department—to name but a few. But cooperation didn't end with officials; it included the public, too, to be genuinely effective.

The Maritime Security Response Team—specialized tactical force of the U.S. Coast Guard.

The boarding of boats is commonplace for the U.S. Coast Guard. Here, a boarding team has terminated the voyage of two commercial fishing vessels for safety violations.

Minutemen and Minutewomen

Ron Wakeham, Fire Chief in Des Moines, IA, at the time of the attacks, laughs wryly as he compares the current buzz with that surrounding the "Minutemen" of the Revolutionary War—ready at a minute's notice to go off and fight the British. He planned to take on 18 new firefighters in 2002, he told the *Christian Science Monitor,* and he expected more than 600 applicants for the positions. Since September 11, 2001, we have been forced to rethink what heroism means and consider the many different ways in which American men and women might defend their country. Teachers coaching their classes in preparedness, veterinarians spotting the signs of what might be the deliberate infection of livestock herds, alert bus drivers, suspicious shopkeepers—all might find themselves in the position of being first responders. The need for all of us to make a contribution to the nation's defense is only underlined by recent indications that the National Guard (the direct successors of the Minutemen) may have been taking on too much.

Many of those who are public spirited enough to volunteer as Guardsmen and -women are already serving as police and prison officers, firefighters, and EMTs. As a result, their **mobilization** has sometimes had the effect of jeopardizing the strength of those agencies in which they normally work. These are early days, of course, and there is no doubt that such difficulties will be ironed out. For instance, the Transportation Security Administration took over the task of ensuring airport security. Having stepped into the breach at a crucial time while the new agency's officers were being recruited and trained, the National Guard turned its attentions to other areas, such as offering assistance to the Border Patrol. There is no doubting the **competence**, commitment, and courage of those already taking on the defense of our country—but the need is clear for all Americans to play their part.

Text-Dependent Questions

1. What is interoperability among first responders?
2. What is the National Data Exchange?
3. What are EMTs and what services do they provide?

Research Projects

1. Research the role of EMTs in emergency situations today. What is their primary mission? How do they accomplish this mission?
2. Research how first responders today coordinate their efforts. What are the top ways they work together?

CHAPTER 4

BEHIND THE SCENES

The seal of the Information Awareness Office— the motto "scientia est potentia" is Latin for knowledge is power.

America's first responders are entitled to every bit of praise that has been heaped upon them in recent months. Yet we should avoid romanticizing action at the expense of **assiduous** intelligence gathering and organization. In any case, no amount of physical courage will protect our financial markets against a terrorist-inspired computer crash; nor will gung-ho heroics prevent hackers from contriving a large-scale shutdown in our power supplies. America's intelligence agencies will have to work hand in hand with law enforcement and rescue services to ensure total readiness against any threat. It is up to the Department of Homeland Security to make sure all these organizations are pulling together.

From Information to Action

In **liaison** with the intelligence services of our allies, the Central Intelligence Agency (CIA) has a role in gathering information about our terrorist enemies. Other agencies—from state and city police departments to the Border Patrol—also have their part to play in the task of intelligence gathering, but the job of interpreting such information falls to the specialist services. The ultimate object of such investigations is, of course, to anticipate the actions of these groups and prevent them if possible.

Words to Understand

Assiduous: Showing great care, attention, and effort.

Liaison: Person who helps organizations or groups work together.

Oppression: Unjust or cruel exercise of power.

Covert counterterrorist operations will be mounted against targets of this kind in order to preempt attack. By their very nature, these operations will remain shadowy; we shall hear little about them. What will remain important is "HUMINT," or human intelligence—information gathered by individual agents using the cloak-and-dagger methods of conventional espionage. Just as important is "SIGINT," or signals information, especially in an age when we can intercept Internet intelligence and emails.

The Information Awareness Office (IAO) was established in 2002, headed by former National Security Adviser Admiral John M. Poindexter. It was equipped to identify terrorist communications along domestic telephone and email networks. After privacy concerns were voiced from many quarters, including the general public, the agency was defunded in 2003. Today these functions are performed by N-DEX and other computer programs. For example, the FBI began surveillance on social media sites, such as Instagram, Facebook, and Twitter, beginning in 2012. Software scans these sites for specific words and phrases, such as ISIS, so agents are alerted to possible attacks or those who may have been part of an attack that has taken place.

However, many people are still concerned about what this type of surveillance means for citizens' rights to privacy. In a March 2015 Pew Research survey, 52 percent of the Americans surveyed were either very concerned or somewhat concerned about the government's surveillance systems.

Introduction to Homeland Security Investigations (ICE).

A Scale of Readiness

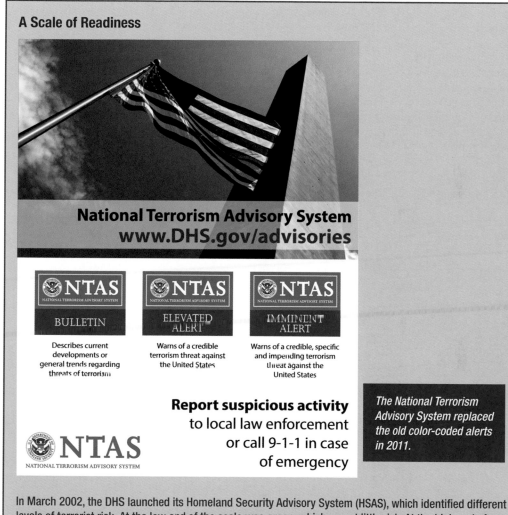

National Terrorism Advisory System
www.DHS.gov/advisories

NTAS
NATIONAL TERRORISM ADVISORY SYSTEM

BULLETIN

Describes current developments or general trends regarding threats of terrorism

NTAS
NATIONAL TERRORISM ADVISORY SYSTEM

ELEVATED ALERT

Warns of a credible terrorism threat against the United States

NTAS
NATIONAL TERRORISM ADVISORY SYSTEM

IMMINENT ALERT

Warns of a credible, specific and impending terrorism threat against the United States

Report suspicious activity
to local law enforcement
or call 9-1-1 in case
of emergency

NTAS
NATIONAL TERRORISM ADVISORY SYSTEM

The National Terrorism Advisory System replaced the old color-coded alerts in 2011.

In March 2002, the DHS launched its Homeland Security Advisory System (HSAS), which identified different levels of terrorist risk. At the low end of the scale was green, which meant little risk. At the high end of the scale was red, which meant a severe risk. In 2011, the DHS replaced that color-coded system with the National Terrorism Advisory System, which acts much like the National Weather Service, issuing two types of advisories when needed to communicate and provide information when there are heightened levels of security risk. The first type of advisory is the bulletin. Bulletins provide stakeholders and the public with information about terrorist threats that may not be necessarily against the United States. Alerts involve specific threats against the United States, and there are two types: elevated (DHS has credible but general information about timing and target) or imminent (DHS has information leading the agency to believe the threat is credible, specific, and impending.)

Combating Human Trafficking at DHS

The mission of the Department of Homeland Security (DHS) is to safeguard the American people, our homeland, and our values. The mission is huge and includes not just safeguarding against terrorism, but also terrible crimes like human trafficking, also known as modern slavery.

In 2010, DHS created the Blue Campaign to serve as the unified voice for its efforts to fight human trafficking. The Blue Campaign has led anti-human trafficking training for law enforcement, federal employees, human trafficking task forces, private sector industry, international audiences, and communities. DHS has trained thousands of people across the United States, including law enforcement, and created a nationwide awareness campaign to raise public consciousness of human trafficking. Through public service announcements, digital media, and advertising at airports, gas stations, and truck stops, the Blue Campaign has empowered communities to recognize and report trafficking.

During the Obama Administration, Immigration and Customs Enforcement Homeland Security Investigations (ICE HSI) initiated more than 6,500 trafficking cases and identified more than 2,000 victims of trafficking. In 2016 alone, ICE HSI, initiated 1,025 human trafficking cases, resulting in 1,943 criminal arrests and 587 convictions, and identified 435 victims of trafficking.

IT at Risk

It is possible that tomorrow's terrorist attack will be carried out invisibly. American inventors and technicians have led the world in developing information technology (IT), finding ways of using computers to organize just about every imaginable aspect of our lives. From water supply and sewage treatment to electricity distribution and street lighting; from telecommunications to traffic lights; from airplane navigation systems to food preparation—all are now managed for us by advanced computer systems. There is hardly any area of life on which IT does not impinge. The benefits are incalculable. So, too, however, are the potential risks. Are we putting too many of our eggs in the IT basket? The more complete our dependency, the greater our vulnerability.

A Cyber Security Campaign

Stop.Think.Connect.™ is a Department of Homeland Security national public awareness campaign aimed at increasing the understanding of cyber threats and empowering the American public to be safer and more secure online. The campaign's main objective is to help people become more aware of growing cyber threats and arm them with the tools to protect themselves, their families, and communities.

Stop.Think.Connect.™ is a national public awareness campaign aimed at increasing the understanding of cyber threats and empowering the American public to be safer and more secure online.

STOP.
Before you use the Internet, take time to understand the risks and learn how to spot potential problems.

THINK.
Take a moment to be certain the path ahead is clear. Watch for warning signs and consider how your actions online could impact your safety, or your family's.

CONNECT.
Enjoy the Internet with greater confidence, knowing you've taken the right steps to safeguard yourself and your computer.

STOP.THINK.CONNECT.
Securing one citizen, one family, one Nation against cyber threats.

Visit *www.dhs.gov/stopthinkconnect* for more information on how to get involved with the Stop.Think.Connect. Campaign.

There have already been several scares, from the mischievous exploits of high school hackers to the more damaging introduction of corrosive viruses that invade information systems and impede or destroy them. Then there are the organized criminal groups using such technology for the purposes of committing fraud or theft on an enormous scale. Finally, of course, there is the threat of sabotage by terrorists. Potentially, at least, such groups could wreak untold havoc in our society, creating meltdown in our financial system and bringing our economy to its knees. Moreover, government and social administration have come to depend strongly on such technologies. Computer systems hold everything from police and prison records to social security data.

Since 2001, two primary developments have created new potential security threats. First, the activist or "hactivist" hacker group called Anonymous. This is a very loosely organized group of hackers that don't have a centralized goal or mission, other than the **oppression** of freedom of speech and in-

formation. One example of their handiwork occurred during the 2016 presidential election when Anonymous claimed it had hacked the computer of the Republican nominee, Donald Trump, and revealed his Social Security number, cell phone number, and additional information. FBI agents are pursuing the group with charges of cyber-stalking, computer hacking, and fraud.

An aerial view of the Pentagon—the Department of Defense headquarters.

Perhaps even more dangerous is the dark, or deep, Web, places on the Internet that are not part of public searches and that few people know how to gain entrance to. The U.S. Pentagon believes ISIS uses the dark Web to recruit new members and to plan real-world attacks. In 2015, the Pentagon launched its MEMEX technology, which can see patterns of activity on the dark Web.

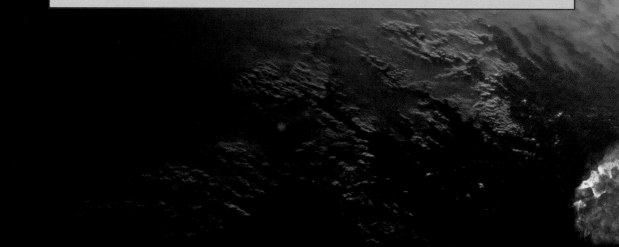

Preparing for a Possible Asteroid Impact

The threat of a huge asteroid hitting the Earth is a favorite plot device in Hollywood disaster movies. Although the scenario is very unlikely, it is possible. The Federal Emergency Management Agency (FEMA) takes the threat seriously, and they have teamed up with scientists at the National Aeronautics and Space Administration (NASA) to try to prepare.

While FEMA would be the agency in charge of the U.S. government efforts in preparing for and responding to any anticipated asteroid-related event here on Earth, NASA is responsible for finding, tracking, and characterizing potentially hazardous asteroids and comets while they are still in space.

Considering how closely FEMA and NASA would need to work together in the event of a potential impact, the two agencies have held several exercises to work through asteroid impact scenarios and simulate the exchange of information from NASA's scientists to FEMA's emergency managers.

Keep the Faith

The attacks of September 2001 tested America's courage—and found it strong and true. Increasingly, however, our longer-term resolve is still in question. The fight for homeland security will be costly, not only in financial terms. In many ways, it has meant an end to the easygoing way of life we had previously enjoyed: extra time in airport lines, additional ID required in offices or banks, intrusive questions from wary public officials. It may now take nothing more than an inconsiderately parked car or a misdirected package to trigger a full-scale security alert. We have gotten used to a certain level of disruption and frustration. Ninety-nine times out of 100, it turns out to be a false alarm, and public patience is tried to its limits. What makes matters worse is that these frustrations bring no immediately obvious benefit—for there is nothing striking or memorable about a terrorist outrage that does not happen. Paradoxically, the more successful the Department of Homeland Security is, the less it will have to show for its work.

It is up to us as Americans to hold our nerve and keep the faith. There will undoubtedly be major benefits to us all, not only in the prevention of future terrorist attacks but also because this is a chance for Americans to come together and build a better, stronger society, if we continue to remain strong and united against terrorism. There may be other benefits too. Health care workers and hospitals geared up to respond swiftly and efficiently to the first signs of bioterrorist attack are likely to deal more effectively with naturally originating outbreaks of infectious disease. The establishment of a "smart border," open to vital commerce but sealed against illegal imports, helps protect our society not only from terrorist weapons but also from illegal drugs. All in all, as President Bush put it, "Homeland security will make America not only stronger, but, in many ways, better."

A member of the Wisconsin National Guard monitors the U.S.–Mexico border from a Border Patrol Station in Arizona.

Text-Dependent Questions

1. What is HUMINT?
2. What is the National Terrorism Advisory System?
3. What is the dark Web?

Research Projects

1. Research N-DEX. How many law enforcement agencies use it and how effective has it been?
2. Research MEMEX technology. Who created it? How many organizations use it? How has it led to increased homeland security?

Series Glosssary

Air marshal: Armed guard traveling on an aircraft to protect the passengers and crew; the air marshal is often disguised as a passenger.

Annexation: To incorporate a country or other territory within the domain of a state.

Armory: A supply of arms for defense or attack.

Assassinate: To murder by sudden or secret attack, usually for impersonal reasons.

Ballistic: Of or relating to firearms.

Biological warfare: Also known as germ warfare, this is war fought with biotoxins—harmful bacteria or viruses that are artificially propagated and deliberately dispersed to spread sickness among an enemy.

Cartel: A combination of groups with a common action or goal.

Chemical warfare: The use of poisonous or corrosive substances to kill or incapacitate the enemy; it differs from biological warfare in that the chemicals concerned are not organic, living germs.

Cold War: A long and bitter enmity between the United States and the Free World and the Soviet Union and its Communist satellites, which went on from 1945 to the collapse of Communism in 1989.

Communism: A system of government in which a single authoritarian party controls state-owned means of production.

Conscription: Compulsory enrollment of persons especially for military service.

Consignment: A shipment of goods or weapons.

Contingency operations: Operations of a short duration and most often performed at short notice, such as dropping supplies into a combat zone.

Counterintelligence: Activities designed to collect information about enemy espionage and then to thwart it.

Covert operations: Secret plans and activities carried out by spies and their agencies.

Cyberterrorism: A form of terrorism that seeks to cause disruption by interfering with computer networks.

Democracy: A government elected to rule by the majority of a country's people.

Depleted uranium: One of the hardest known substances, it has most of its radioactivity removed before being used to make bullets.

Dissident: A person who disagrees with an established religious or political system, organization, or belief.

Embargo: A legal prohibition on commerce.

Emigration: To leave one country to move to another country.

Extortion: The act of obtaining money or other property from a person by means of force or intimidation.

Extradite: To surrender an alleged criminal from one state or nation to another having jurisdiction to try the charge.

Federalize/federalization: The process by which National Guard units, under state command in normal circumstances, are called up by the president in times of crisis to serve the federal government of the United States as a whole.

Genocide: The deliberate and systematic destruction of a racial, political, or cultural group.

Guerrilla: A person who engages in irregular warfare, especially as a member of an independent unit carrying out harassment and sabotage.

Hijack: To take unlawful control of a ship, train, aircraft, or other form of transport.

Immigration: The movement of a person or people ("immigrants") into a country; as opposed to emigration, their movement out.

Indict: To charge with a crime by the finding or presentment of a jury (as a grand jury) in due form of law.

Infiltrate: To penetrate an organization, like a terrorist network.

Infrastructure: The crucial networks of a nation, such as transportation and communication, and also including government organizations, factories, and schools.

Insertion: Getting into a place where hostages are being held.

Insurgent: A person who revolts against civil authority or an established government.

Internment: To hold someone, especially an immigrant, while his or her application for residence is being processed.

Logistics: The aspect of military science dealing with the procurement, maintenance, and transportation of military matériel, facilities, and personnel.

Matériel: Equipment, apparatus, and supplies used by an organization or institution.

Militant: Having a combative or aggressive attitude.

Militia: a military force raised from civilians, which supports a regular army in times of war.

Narcoterrorism: Outrages arranged by drug trafficking gangs to destabilize government, thus weakening law enforcement and creating conditions for the conduct of their illegal business.

NATO: North Atlantic Treaty Organization; an organization of North American and European countries formed in 1949 to protect one another against possible Soviet aggression.

Naturalization: The process by which a foreigner is officially "naturalized," or accepted as a U.S. citizen.

Nonstate actor: A terrorist who does not have official government support.

Ordnance: Military supplies, including weapons, ammunition, combat vehicles, and maintenance tools and equipment.

Refugee: A person forced to take refuge in a country not his or her own, displaced by war or political instability at home.

Rogue state: A country, such as Iraq or North Korea, that ignores the conventions and laws set by the international community; rogue states often pose a threat, either through direct military action or by harboring terrorists.

Sortie: One mission or attack by a single plane.

Sting: A plan implemented by undercover police in order to trap criminals.

Surveillance: To closely watch over and monitor situations; the USAF employs many different kinds of surveillance equipment and techniques in its role as an intelligence gatherer.

Truce: A suspension of fighting by agreement of opposing forces.

UN: United Nations; an international organization, of which the United States is a member, that was established in 1945 to promote international peace and security.

Chronology

1917: The Russian Revolution involved the overthrow of the tyrannical government of the czars in favor of what would turn out to be the more oppressive government of the Communist leaders.

1926: Mussolini, a fascist dictator, comes to power in Italy.

1933: Adolf Hitler comes to power in Germany; over the next few years, his National Socialist, or Nazi, party establishes an iron grip over every section of government and society.

1939: September 1, German forces invade Poland, initiating the European phase of World War II.

1941: December 7, Germany's Axis ally, Japan, mounts a surprise attack on the U.S. fleet lying in Pearl Harbor; the United States is brought into what is now genuinely a world war.

1945: World War II comes to an end and the Cold War between the free West and Communist Eastern Europe and China begins.

1948: The state of Israel is founded in the aftermath of Hitler's Holocaust, but the new nation finds itself threatened by its Arab neighbors.

1979: The Iranian Revolution overthrows the shah, and Muslim fanatics take control; this represents a decisive moment in the rise of Islamic fundamentalism.

1989: The Soviet Union collapses, exhausted by a 10-year war in Afghanistan and drained by years of economic stagnation and administrative inefficiency.

1990: Forces of Iraqi dictator Saddam Hussein invade neighboring Kuwait; in the ensuing Gulf War (1991), the aggressors are expelled, but the U.S.-led alliance stops short of interfering in the affairs of a sovereign state to the extent of actually deposing its leader.

1995: March 20, members of the Aum Shinri Kyo ("Supreme Truth") cult mount a sarin nerve-gas attack on the Tokyo subway; April 19, Oklahoma City bombing highlights the threat posed by "patriots" for whom the federal government is an enemy of (white) America.

2001: September 11, Members of the terrorist group Al Qaeda fly hijacked airliners into the twin towers of the World Trade Center, New York, and into the Pentagon, Washington, DC;

a fourth jet crashes in Pennsylvania after passengers overpower the hijackers; October 8, the Office of Homeland Security is established by President George W. Bush.

2002: President Bush establishes the Citizen Corps to mobilize voluntary action for homeland security at the community level; the Border Security and Visa Entry Reform Act is passed to tighten controls on America's borders.

2005: Michael Chertoff is appointed Homeland Security Secretary.

2011: DHS launches the National Terrorism Advisory System.

2009: Janet Napolitano is appointed Homeland Security Secretary.

2013: Jeh Johnson is appointed Homeland Security Secretary.

2015: Government announces that in June more than 10 individuals with ties to Islamic State—also known as ISIS or ISIL—were arrested across the country.

2017: John F. Kelly is appointed Homeland Security Secretary.

Further Resources

The National Citizens' Crime Prevention Campaign has responded specifically to the terrorist alert of recent times to produce a series of media advertisements aimed at heightening general awareness and alertness. Its slogan is "United for a Stronger America." In conjunction with the government, it has published a free booklet offering sensible advice. You can get a copy of the *United for a Stronger America: Citizens Preparedness Guide* simply by calling the toll-free number: 1-800-WEPREVENT.

Websites

For the latest news and information on homeland security, see: www.whitehouse.gov/news/releases

For the Anser Institute for Homeland Security, see: www.homelanddefense.org/bulletin

Try this site if you would like to make a contribution toward the defense of the United States: www.citizencorps.gov

For the National Homeland Security Knowledgebase—the definitive site for homeland security information, see: www.twotigersonline.com/resources

To learn more about cybersecurity, see: www.dhs.gov/topic/cybersecurity

Further Reading

Armstrong, Karen. *Islam: A Short History.* New York: Modern Library, 2000.

Hoge, James F., Jr., and Gideon Rose. *How Did This Happen? Terrorism and the New War.* New York: Public Affairs, 2001.

Daalder, Ivo H., I. M. Destler, Robert E. Litan, Michael E. O'Hanlon, and Peter Orszag. *Achieving Homeland Security.* Washington, DC: Brookings Institution, 2002.

Nemeth, Charles P. *Homeland Security: An Introduction to Principles and Practice,* 2nd ed. Boca Raton, FL: CRC Press, 2013.

Philpott, Don. *Understanding the Department of Homeland Security.* New York: Berman Press, 2015.

Index

About the Author

Michael Kerrigan was born in Liverpool, England, and educated at St. Edward's College, from where he won an Open Scholarship to University College, Oxford. He lived for a time in the United States, spending time first at Princeton, followed by a period working in publishing in New York. Since then he has been a freelance writer and journalist, with commissions across a very wide range of subjects, but with a special interest in social policy and defense issues. Within this field, he has written on every region of the world. His work has been published by leading international educational publishers, including the BBC, Dorling Kindersley, Time-Life, and Reader's Digest Books. His work as a journalist includes regular contributions to the *Times Literary Supplement,* London, as well as a weekly column in the *Scotsman* newspaper, Edinburgh, where he now lives with his wife and their two small children.

About the Consultant

Manny Gomez, an expert on terrorism and security, is President of MG Security Services and a former Principal Relief Supervisor and Special Agent with the FBI. He investigated terrorism and espionage cases as an agent in the National Security Division. He was a certified undercover agent and successfully completed Agent Survival School. Chairman of the Board of the National Law Enforcement Association (NLEA), Manny is also a former Sergeant in the New York Police Department (NYPD) where he supervised patrol and investigative activities of numerous police officers, detectives and civilian personnel. Mr. Gomez worked as a uniformed and plainclothes officer in combating narcotics trafficking, violent crimes, and quality of life concerns. He has executed over 100 arrests and received Departmental recognition on eight separate occasions. Mr. Gomez has a Bachelor's Degree and Master's Degree and is a graduate of Fordham University School of Law where he was on the Dean's list. He is admitted to the New York and New Jersey Bar. He served honorably in the United States Marine Corps infantry.